CHESS LEGENDS ALPHABET

Words by Robin Feiner

A is for Maurice **A**shley. This Jamaican-born US Chess Hall of Famer is the first Black grandmaster to grace the sport. His reach stretches far beyond his playing wizardry, too: He's a renowned chess commentator, author, and teacher, even founding the Harlem Chess Center in 1999.

B is for Mikhail **B**otvinnik. Before Kasparov, the face of the Russian chess revolution was Botvinnik. With an iron will and fierce strategic planning, he became a three-time world champ. He played chess at the highest level for over 30 years, ultimately leading to his nickname, 'The Father of Soviet Chess.'

C is for Maia **C**hiburdanidze. At 17, Chiburdanidze became the youngest female world champ in chess history, a record at the time. She won 14 gold medals in Chess Olympiads and was the second female grandmaster ever. Most importantly, she ushered in a new era of chess in her home nation of Georgia.

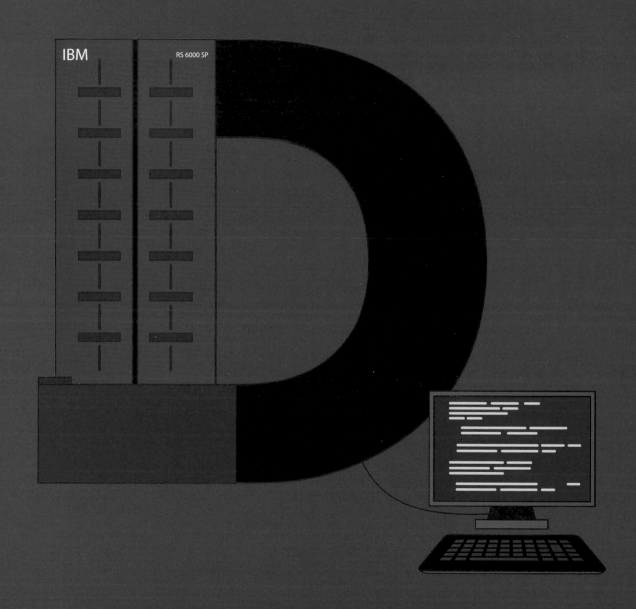

D is for Deep Blue.
This chess-playing super-
computer aimed to provide
one final answer to the
ultimate question: 'Man or
machine?' After losing to
the great Garry Kasparov
in 1989 and '96, Deep Blue
returned bigger and better
in '97, besting Kasparov in
a battle for the ages.

Ee

E is for Emanuel Lasker.
A relentless attacker,
Lasker toyed with his
opponents by intentionally
playing inferior moves. His
crowning glory came when
he defeated Wilhelm Steinitz
to become the second-ever
chess world champion. He
held this title for 27 years—
the longest reign in history.

F is for Bobby **F**ischer. Before beating Spassky in their famous Cold War matchup of 1972, Fischer helped revitalize chess in America. He's one of the greatest prodigies the sport has ever seen, a tactical maestro, and a legendary fighter until the end.

G is for Nona Gaprindashvili. In 1978, this Georgia-born legend and women's world champion became the first female grandmaster in chess history. She's still going strong in her 80s, having won another seniors' world championship in 2022 at the ripe age of 81.

H is for **H**ikaru Nakamura. Nakamura, a Japanese-American legend, started young and has never looked back. By the age of 15 he had stolen Fischer's crown as the youngest grandmaster in US history. Now he's an ace of speed and classical variants and a five-time US chess champ.

I is for Vasyl **I**vanchuk. This legend has beaten some of the greats, including Karpov and Carlsen. The Ukrainian 'Chuky' is known in chess circles for his dramatic style. He'll sacrifice pawns out of nowhere, throwing off foes just long enough for him to topple their king and claim victory.

J is for Judit Polgár.
Her future was obvious
the moment she crushed a
master, blindfolded, at the
age of seven. Before retiring
in 2014, this Hungarian
legend dominated the
women's side while also
beating 11 male world
champs. Polgár is the
GOAT of women's chess.

K is for Garry **K**asparov. This legendary Russian grandmaster is the king of checkmates. He beat a supercomputer, dominated the sport for two-plus decades, and won a record 11 Best Chess Player of the Year awards. Kasparov is one of the greatest ever to wield a rook, pawn, or knight.

L is for Jessica T. **L**auser. Visually impaired from birth, the American Lauser took up chess as a hobby. Her interest grew in school while escaping her bullies. Now, she's a five-time US Blind Chess Champion and an indisputable legend, earning her the nickname 'Chessica.'

M is for **M**agnus Carlsen. The 'Mozart of Chess,' was just five years old when he first played, and he's been chipping away at records ever since. By 13, he was a grandmaster; by 15, Norwegian Chess Champion; and by 19, the world's top-ranked player – the youngest ever to get there. Look out, Kasparov!

N is for Natan Sharansky. After finding himself in prison, this Israeli played chess every day to keep him from going insane. But he had no board or pieces—he played only in his mind, against himself! One day, in 1996, he sat down across a chess board from Kasparov and won.

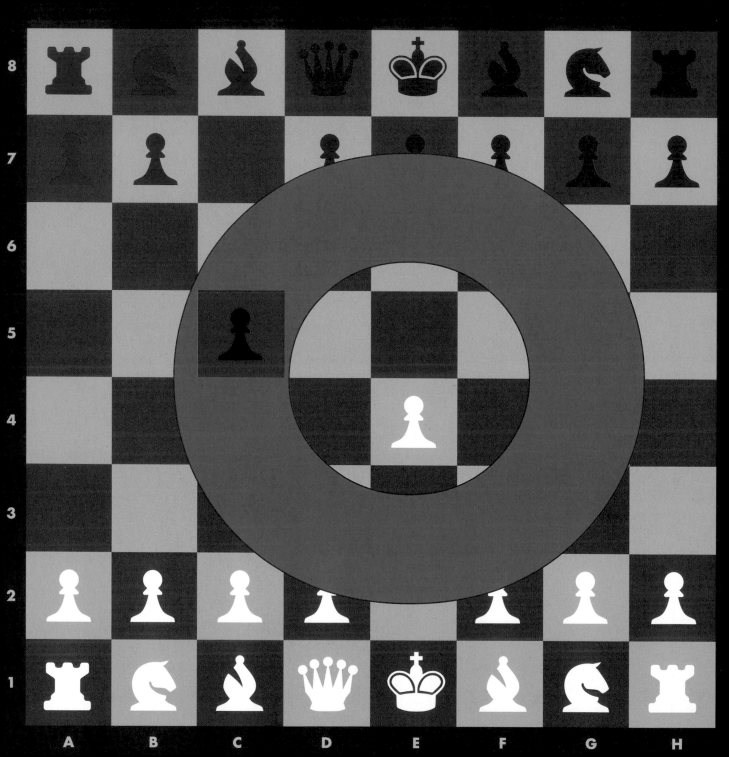

Oo

O is for Sicilian Defense opening. Chess is a game of strategy, and no move is more dynamic than Polerio's legendary 16th-century opening. The Sicilian Defense is an opening weapon used by grandmasters and amateurs alike to defend their king and stage a counterattack.

P is for Paul Morphy.
As a child, Morphy was regarded as the best chess player in New Orleans. At just nine years old, he skillfully defeated a top American army general, and was celebrated as the US's first chess prodigy. He went on to become the best player in the world at the time.

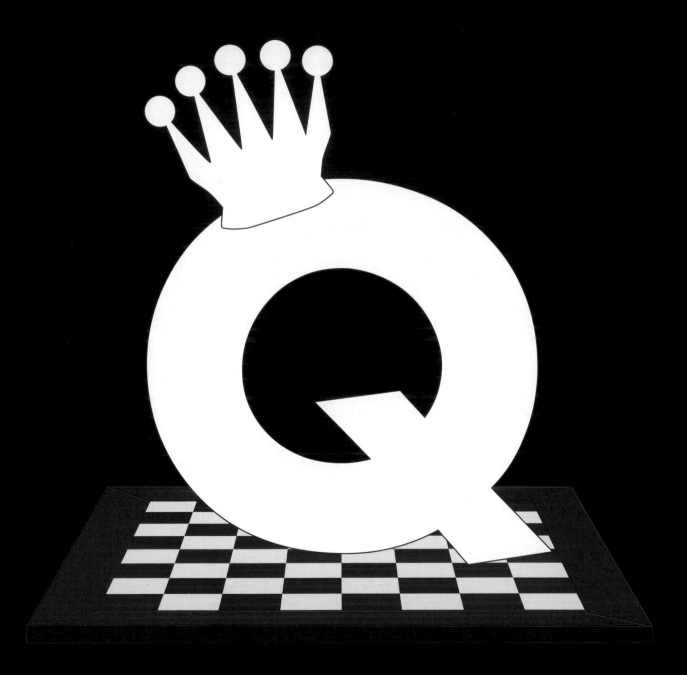

Qq

Q is for The Queen.
She can move side to side,
forward and back, and
diagonally too. When her
immense power is wielded
correctly, all other pieces
fall in her wake. The Queen
is the ultimate piece, the
breaker of ties, the black or
white goddess who strikes
the final blow. 'Checkmate.'

R is for José **R**aúl Capablanca. From 1916-24, the 'Human Chess Machine' didn't lose a single match. Capablanca was a Cuban wrecking ball known for his tactical abilities, endgame skills, and speed of play. Nobody sprang the dreaded 'zwischenzug' move on opponents quite like he did.

Ss

S is for Amon Simutowe. Though he once dreamed of playing for Zambia's national soccer team, Simutowe's calling as a chess master was too hard to ignore. In 2007, he became chess history's third Black grandmaster after toppling the great Nakamura.

T is for **T**igran Petrosian. Orphaned as a boy, this Soviet-Armenian lad swept streets to earn a living. Thankfully, 'Iron Tigran's' rough upbringing led him to develop a renowned defensive style on the chess board. With his impenetrable defense he became the 1963 and '66 world champion.

U is for Sergey **U**rusov. The Urusov Gambit in the Bishop's Opening is named after this chess legend. He was a friend to Leo Tolstoy, an officer in the Russian army, and a member of Russian nobility. Devoting his life to chess, he became one of Russia's best 19th-century players.

Vv

V is for **V**era Menchik.
As the first Women's World Chess Champion, Vera dominated the sport with an epic 17-year run from 1927 to '44. She also pushed for the acceptance of women playing in male tournaments. Menchik was a legend who paved the way for all those who followed.

MODERN
CHESS
INSTRUCTOR

PART I

W. STEINITZ

Ww

W is for **W**ilhelm Steinitz. Becoming the first ever World Chess Champion in 1886, Steinitz is credited with revolutionizing the game, earning him the name 'the father of modern chess.' He shifted focus from attack to a more strategic style, making chess a more thoughtful, graceful game.

X is for Han **Xin.**
Some say chess was invented in the 6th century BC, while others claim it was later. Many enthusiasts believe that Han Xin, the Chinese war Commander, started the beautiful game around 200 BC. He used a 64 square chess board to display his ingenious war tactics, and the rest is history.

Y is for Hou Yifan.
This Chinese prodigy took
up chess when she was only
three. By nine, she was a
world youth champion,
and by 14, she'd become
the youngest female grand-
master ever. The only
question left is whether
she can top Polgar as the
greatest female chess
player of all time.

Z is for Johannes **Z**ukertort. An avid blindfolded player and amazing strategist, this Polish legend was known for his unexpected sacrifices and killer finishes. The London 1883 Chess Tournament is remembered as his greatest victory, as he came to beat Wilhelm Steinitz, his long-standing rival.